The Wonderful Story Of God's Plan For Jesus

Written and Illustrated by R. Cherie Lepeak

James Kay Publishing

Tulsa, Oklahoma

The Wonderful Story of God's Plan for Jesus
ISBN 978-1-943245-67-3

www.jameskaypublishing.com

e-mail: sales@jameskaypublishing.com

© 2021 Cherie Lepeak
Cover Art & Illustrations by Cherie Lepeak
Author Photo by Steve Lepeak

A Note From The Author

It all started forty years ago, I was twenty-two then. I watched my parents struggling to get their homework done as they attended the Bristol Road School of Biblical Studies in Flint Michigan. I was a young mother of two and although I was very proud of their undertaking, I just wanted their attention on my little ones instead of their noses in their studies.

After my parents graduated from the school, it wasn't until years later that I felt the full impact of what they had learned.

My Dad preached and later became and elder of the Church. My Mother used her knowledge to be a ladies' Bible class teacher. But the things they were teaching were different and amazing! I'd never heard the Bible taught with such clarity! It was very exciting to me as I sat in my Mother's class.

Soon after our lessons were concluded, one of the elder's wives approached my Mother and said she had never heard anything like this taught before. She said it opened her eyes about the Bible being one story with one plan. She then proceeded to tell my Mother she should write her lessons in a book form so others could pass on what she was teaching.

That started the ball rolling. One of my sisters, Kellie, and I worked side-by-side with my Mother for about a year. We typed, gathered her illustrations, and continued to type until finally her class study book was created! The title is *Redemption Through Jesus, Planned, Prophesied and Fulfilled* by Rita G. Draper. Since then her book has been taught in many classrooms all across the country.

A few years later, I volunteered to teach our ladies' Bible class and decided to teach my Mother's book. I was scared as I had only taught children before. But as I taught, our preacher's wife told me she had never heard teaching like this before. She said it made the Bible so understandable and gave purpose to all the Old Testament stories connecting them to the New Testament as one story! She was so excited!

Soon after I finished teaching the ladies' Bible class on Tuesdays, I took my turn teaching our Sunday morning Children's class. Because we were a small congregation, I taught ages five through eleven. It was a challenge, but I love challenges!

As I thought about what to teach the children, I decided to teach them what the ladies had learned only on a children's level.

As I wrote and needed specific illustrations, I just created my own. Everyone got such a kick out of my art work! That was the start of writing this book *The Wonderful Story of God's Plan for Jesus*.

When I finished this book, I read it to a few of my older grandchildren. They loved it and asked if I could write another book for teenagers. I said, "Of course!" and started writing my second book, *God Has our Backs, Making Sense of the Bible for Teens*.

My desire is to teach young people the things I never knew as a young Christian. Two of the things being the blessing of knowing the Bible as one complete story and the assurance of having a home with God forever when we die.

I know you will love reading this book, giving it as a gift, or sharing it with friends or neighbors. Give hope in this world to someone you love!

In Christian Love,

With all my heart,

R. Cherie Lepeak

Instructions for Reading This Book

This entire book comes from another very special book that is called the Bible. The <u>Bible</u> is filled with God's own Words! Our book is like a puzzle fitting all the chapters together as pieces of God's plan for Jesus. God planned for Jesus to come to earth and save us from the naughty things we do called sins. That way, after we die, we will be able to go to Heaven and live with God, Jesus, and the angels for ever and ever. How exciting that will be for us!

As you read this book you will see a picture of a small puzzle piece at the beginning of each chapter. Each puzzle piece will be a story part of the plan God made for Jesus.

When you finish the last chapter, there will be a page with all the puzzle pieces on it. You may cut them out, or make a copy of the page to cut, and put your puzzle pieces together making the picture of Jesus!

When reading our story look for the picture of the girl reading the Bible that appears in each chapter. At the end of the chapter there will be a section called:

"Finding God's Plan in His Book"

Match the story girls to the girls in this section to find where that part of our story is found in God's Word, the Bible.

At the very beginning of each chapter you will see the following picture marking the section called: "In a Nut Shell"

In this section you will find a short summary of everything we've learned so far in,

"The Wonderful Story of God's Plan for Jesus"

Enjoy!

Contents

A Note From The Author v

Instructions for Reading this Book.. vii

Acknowledgements... x

Chapter 1 The Beginning of God's Plan.................................... 1

Chapter 2 Noah, Part of God's Plan....................................... 5

Chapter 3 Abraham, Part of God's Plan with Promises............ 11

Chapter 4 The Huge Family Started with 12 Sons.................... 17

Chapter 5 Joseph, One of the 12, Part of God's Plan................ 23

Chapter 6 Joseph Saves his Family From Starving................... 29

Chapter 7 Moses, The Baby in God's Plan............................... 37

Chapter 8 Moses, The Man in God's Plan................................ 45

Chapter 9 King David in God's Plan.. 57

Chapter 10 God's Plan Finally Brought Jesus.......................... 65

Chapter 11 Jesus Is Baptized by John the Baptist.................... 71

Chapter 12 Jesus Chooses 12 Helpers......................................77

Chapter 13 Jesus Dies on the Cross and Is Alive Again............. 83

Chapter 14 The First People in Jesus' Church......................... 89

Puzzle of Jesus.. 95

Acknowledgements

This book was written with the hope of furthering the
message of the Bible to all children. Even though targeting children,
this book is great reading for all ages. It will take you
through the entire Bible making it as the
one story It was written to be.

My Mother, Rita Draper, wrote the book these chapters originated from.
Her book entitled *Redemption through Christ, Planned,
Prophesied, and Fulfilled*
was written for fifth grade through adult ages to be used as
class material. Her book has been taught in many
classrooms across our country.

Thank you to my Daddy, Garland Draper and Mama, Rita, for being such a great
Christian example and raising me to know our wonderful God.
Thank you to my Husband, Steve, for being supportive and patient while
I worked on writing and creating the illustrations for this book.
I also wish to thank our Children and their spouses,
Chrissy, Aron, Michael, Amanda, Patrick, Megan, Kari, Joe, and Steven.
I also wish to thank our 14 Grandchildren, Ethan, Noah, Jade, Lily, Connor,
Liam, Amelia, Colette, Isaac, Zander, Channah, Lucas, Izzy, and Megan,
for being such inspirations to me for writing this book.
Thankyou to my Sisters, Gwen and Kellie, for being so supportive during this endeavor.
Most of all, I wish to thank God for making His plan
to bring Jesus to save us from our sins!
In Christian Love,
R. Cherie Lepeak

Chapter 1
The Beginning of God's Plan

This puzzle piece of our story begins a long, long, time ago. So long ago, that the earth wasn't even here yet. There was only a place called Heaven! The Bible, which is God's Word, tells us that God, His son Jesus, and the angels, all lived in Heaven.

God had an idea to make people and a world for us to live in. But God knew we would all do naughty things called sins. God does not like sin and our sins would not let us go to Heaven when we die. But do not worry God made a plan for us. He would send His son Jesus to our world to save us from our sins! That would make a way for us to go to Heaven too!

In our story, after God made His plan to send Jesus, He made everything in the world! He made the sun, moon, stars, animals, fish, birds, grass, trees, and then He made the first family! God made Adam and Eve!

God made a special beautiful place for Adam and Eve to live. It was called the Garden of Eden! Adam and Eve loved living in the garden. God told them they could eat anything in the garden except from one of the special trees He had made. Tempted by the Devil they disobeyed God and ate from it anyway which was the first sin. God made them leave the garden and never come back. He also told them they had to plant and work for all their food to eat from that time on. God told them to start a family and they had many children. Three of their children were named Cain, Abel, and Seth.

Part of God's plan to send Jesus was for Seth to grow up and get married. Seth and his wife then had babies and grandbabies. Soon Jesus was coming as one of their great, great, great, great, grandbabies! That is why we say, "Jesus was coming from Seth".

This is the start of God's Big Plan!

"Finding God's Plan in His Book"

 God's Plan for us was before the beginning of time.
Ephesians chapter 1 verses 3-5, I Peter chapter 1 verses 20-21

 God made the world and everything in it.
Genesis chapter 1 verses 1-27

 The first family was found in Genesis chapter 2 verse 8,
Genesis 1:28, Genesis 4:1-25

The Genealogy of Jesus is in Luke 3:38

The People God used in His Plan to Bring Jesus!

Adam

Seth

In a Nut Shell

So far in our story God made a plan to bring Jesus to earth to save us from our sins! God made this plan before He made anything else! Jesus is coming from the first family's son named Seth!

Chapter 2
Noah, Part of God's Plan

This Puzzle piece of our story is very exciting! It's about a man named Noah and his family. Noah had a wife, three sons, and they had wives. Noah's sons were named Shem, Ham, and Japheth!

Remember when we talked about the naughty things called sins? Well, when Noah and his family were living on the earth, all the people were doing a lot of sins. Noah and his family were the only ones who still loved God. Imagine how awful the world must have been!

God decided to save Noah and his family and get rid of all the people that did not love Him. Do you know how He did that? God made it rain covering the whole earth with water! But…….God told Noah to build a huge boat called an Ark! God told Noah exactly what kind of wood to use and exactly how big to make the ark. Noah followed God's instructions perfectly!

When it started raining, Noah, his family, and some of the animals went through the big door of the ark. They were all snug as bugs in there safe from all the water outside. It rained and rained! For forty days and forty nights it rained! I wonder if they thought it was never going to stop raining. The water stayed on the earth one hundred fifty days. Finally God made the wind blow and blow and it dried up all the water!

Now that the land was dry again, Noah and his family, and all the animals came out of the Ark! They were so happy to be on dry land after staying in the ark such a long time! It was then that God made a promise to Noah. He told Noah that He would never again get rid of all the people on the earth with a flood. God put a beautiful rainbow in the sky as a reminder to Noah and all of us, of His promise.

Remember God's plan to bring Jesus to the earth? That is why God saved Noah and his family from the flood because Jesus was coming from them. Remember Noah's sons, Shem, Ham, and Japheth? Jesus was going to come from Shem! Shem and his wife would have children and grandchildren, and eventually Jesus would be born!

"Finding God's Plan in His Book"

 Noah's family is in Genesis 6:9 and 10

 Noah's family, the only ones loving God, found in Genesis 6:5-8

 Directions for building the ark are found in Genesis 6:11-16

 Promise of the rainbow found in Genesis 7:6

 Jesus coming from Shem found in Luke 3:36 Genealogy of Jesus

The People God used in His Plan to Bring Jesus!

Adam

Seth

Noah

Shem

The People God used in His Plan to Bring Jesus!

In a Nut Shell

So far in our story God made the plan for Jesus to come to earth and save us from our sins! Jesus was coming from Adam and Eve's son Seth! When the world became wicked, God saved Noah's family in the Ark from the flood, because Jesus was coming from his son Shem!

Chapter 3
Abraham, Part of God's Plan with Promises

This puzzle piece of our story is about a man named Abraham. Remember when God told Noah's family to have lots of children and fill the world with people again? Abraham was one of Shem's great, great, grandchildren. Abraham is part of God's plan to bring Jesus to save us from our sins!

Our story continues as Abraham grew to be a full grown man. He decided to marry a beautiful woman named Sarah. After they had been married for awhile, God spoke to Abraham and made **3 promises** to him.

The **First Promise** God made to Abraham was that he and Sarah would have many children and their family would be huge, as many as the stars in the sky. God said, "I will make you into a great nation." This great nation that God promised was called the Israelites. We will learn much more later in our story about the Israelites.

The **Second Promise** God made to Abraham was, "to your huge family I will give a special land. This land would be the most beautiful land and the name of it would be Canaan."

12

The **Third Promise** God made was that "all people would be blessed through Abraham." "Blessed" means that good things would happen to the people.

The good thing that was going to happen to the people was that Jesus was coming from Abraham. Jesus was going to save us from our sins!

"Finding God's Plan in His Book"

 **1st Promise**: Genesis 12:2 and 15:5 It came true in Genesis 46:3

 **2nd Promise**: Genesis 2:7 It came true in Joshua 21:43

 **3rd Promise**: Genesis 12:3 It came true in Galatians 3:8 and 16.

 Jesus was coming from Abraham in Luke 3:34

The People God used in His Plan to Bring Jesus!

Adam

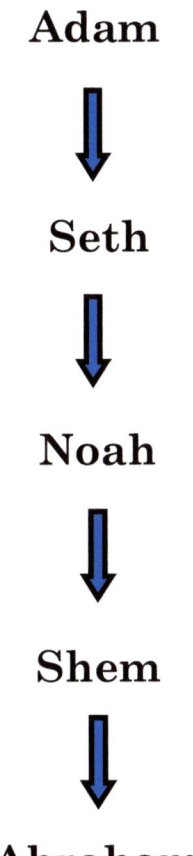

Seth

Noah

Shem

Abraham

In a Nut Shell

So far in our story God plans to bring Jesus to save us from our sins. Jesus was coming from Seth! When the world became wicked, God saved Noah's family from the big flood because Jesus was coming from Shem! God made **3 promises** to Shem's great grandson, Abraham. The **First Promise** was, Abraham would have a huge family. The **Second Promise** was, they would live in Canaan. The **Third Promise** was, all people would be blessed through Abraham because Jesus was coming from him.

Chapter 4
The Huge Family Started With 12 Sons

This piece of the puzzle in our story is about how God's **First Promise** to Abraham started. Remember the **First Promise** was to make Abraham's family huge, as many as the stars?

It all started with Abraham and his wife Sarah. When they were very, very old God promised they would have a son and his name would be Isaac. Sarah laughed about this promise! But guess what? It surprised her that it actually came true! They had a son when they were very, very old and named him Isaac!

Isaac grew and grew! When he became a man, he was married and they had a baby named Jacob. But it didn't stop there!

Jacob grew and grew and was married. They had twelve sons! Their names were Issachar, Zebulun, Levi, Benjamin, Reuben, Simeon, Judah, Dan, Naphtali, Gad, Asher, and Joseph. Wow! That's a great start to the huge family God had promised!

Remember God's plan to bring Jesus to earth to save us from our sins? Which one of the twelve sons of Jacob do you think Jesus was coming from?

It was Judah! Judah grew and grew and soon became a man. He was married and they had children and grandchildren and soon Jesus was coming! So we say Jesus was coming from Judah!

"Finding God's Plan in His Book"

 This story is found in Genesis 29:31 through Genesis 30:22

 Jesus was coming from Judah in Luke 3:33

The People God used in His Plan to Bring Jesus!

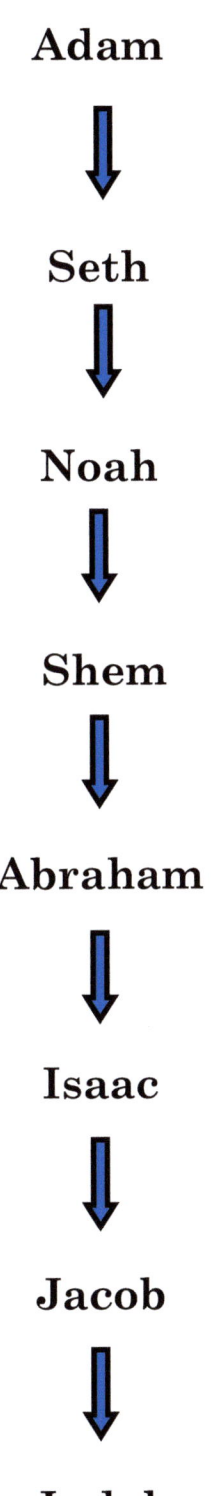

Adam

Seth

Noah

Shem

Abraham

Isaac

Jacob

Judah

In a Nut Shell

In our story so far, God planned to send Jesus to save us from our sins and Jesus was coming from Seth! When the world became wicked, God saved Noah so Jesus could come from his son Shem! Then, God promised Shem's great grandson, Abraham, **3 Promises**. **1.** I will give you a huge family. **2.** They will live in Canaan. **3.** All people will be blessed through you, Jesus is that blessing. God started the **First Promise** coming true with Abraham, Isaac, Jacob, and his 12 sons. Jesus is coming from Judah!

Chapter 5
Joseph, One of the 12! Part of God's Plan

This piece of the puzzle in our story is about one of Jacob's twelve sons named Joseph. Jacob loved Joseph very, very much and gave him a special, beautiful coat of many colors. Joseph's brothers were very jealous of Joseph and his new coat.

One day Joseph's Daddy, Jacob, asked Joseph to go find his brothers. They were watching their sheep eat in a field. So Joseph left in search of his brothers. He finally found them and headed to the field where they were.

When Joseph's brothers saw him coming, they quickly made a plan between themselves to get rid of Joseph. Poor Joseph had no idea what they were planning.

When Joseph walked close enough to his brothers, they grabbed him and threw him into a hole in the ground which was an old dried up well!

Poor Joseph! How would his father or anyone find him in an old dry well!

Later on, the same day, the brothers were eating their lunch. All of a sudden they saw some men coming down the road nearby. The brothers quickly came up with a new plan to get rid of their brother, Joseph. Poor Joseph still had no idea what was about to happen to him!

When the men grew closer to the brothers, they stopped the men. They asked where the men were going and they told the brothers they were on their way to a country called Egypt. That sounded great to the brothers! They made a deal with the men to sell Joseph to them. The men would take Joseph to Egypt. The brothers would finally be rid of Joseph forever!

Please do not worry about Joseph. All the things that are happening to him are all a part of God's plan! It may look bad for Joseph now, but just you wait and see! Wonderful things happen to him while he is living in Egypt! Remember Jesus is coming from Joseph's brother Judah.

"Finding God's Plan in His Book"

 This story is found in Genesis chapter 37

 Jesus was coming from Joseph's brother Judah in Luke 3:33

The People God used in His Plan to Bring Jesus!

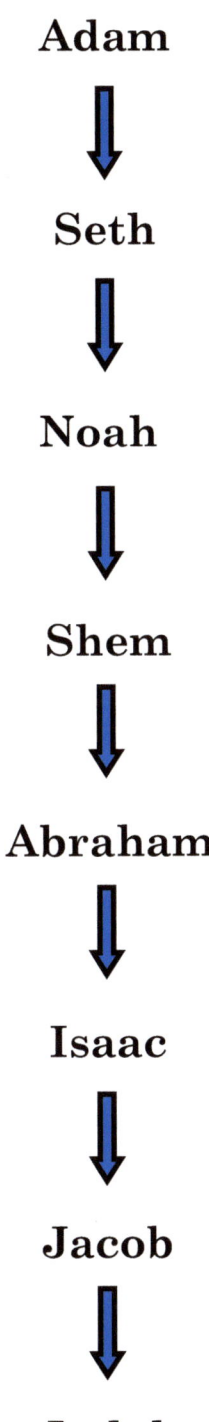

Adam
↓
Seth
↓
Noah
↓
Shem
↓
Abraham
↓
Isaac
↓
Jacob
↓
Judah

In a Nut Shell

So far in our story God is going to bring Jesus to save us from our sins and He is coming from Seth. When the world grew wicked, God saved Noah from the flood so Jesus could come from his son Shem! God promised Shem's great grandson, Abraham, **3 promises**. **1.** You will have a huge family. **2.** They will live in Canaan. **3.** All people on earth will be blessed through you. Jesus was that blessing. God started the **First Promise** coming true with Abraham, Isaac, Jacob, and his 12 sons. Jesus was coming from Judah. Joseph, one of the 12 brothers, was thrown into a well and then sold to men going to Egypt. All because his brothers were jealous of him. God uses Joseph in His plan to bring Jesus!

Chapter 6
Joseph Saves His Family From Starving

In this puzzle piece of our story we read how God used Joseph in His plan while Joseph was in the country called Egypt. It all started with the most important man in Egypt called Pharaoh. He was like a king or like our presidents.

One night while Pharaoh was sleeping, he had a dream. It was about cows and grain. What a strange dream! It was so strange that when Pharaoh woke up that morning, he wanted to know what his dream about the cows and grain meant.

That day Joseph heard about the Pharaoh's dream. Joseph knew that with God's help he could tell the Pharaoh what his dream meant. In fact Joseph was the only one in the whole country of Egypt that could do this.

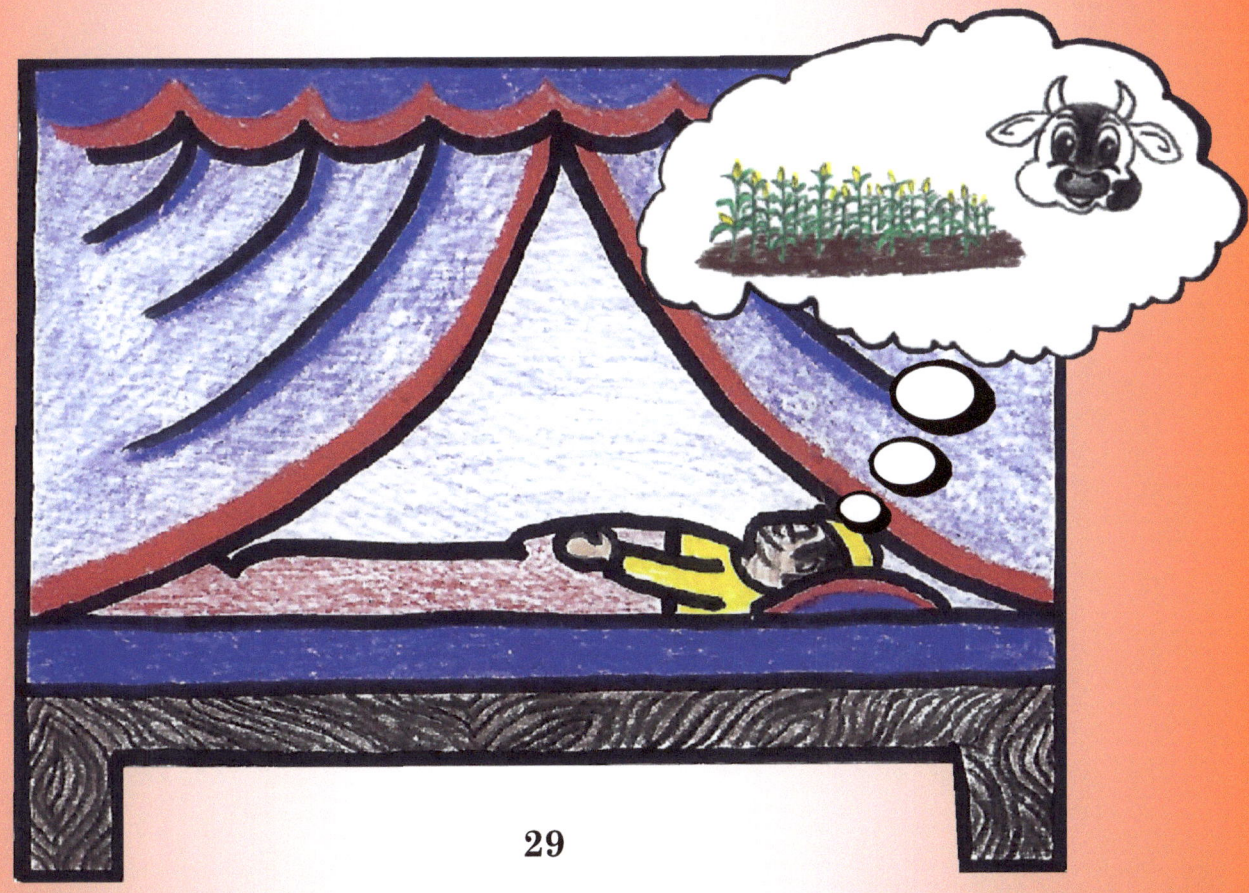

When Joseph came before the Pharaoh, he told him his dream. Pharaoh said, "I dreamed about cows and fields of grain." Joseph then began, with God's help, to tell the Pharaoh what his dream meant. Joseph said that the land and all the people were going to have 7 years of lots of food growing in the fields. Then the next 7 years there would be no food growing at all. This is called a famine.

Pharaoh was happy to know what his dream meant. He was so happy he told Joseph that he would be in charge of all the land of Egypt. Pharaoh also told Joseph that he should save some food every year when there was a lot of food growing for the first seven years. Then when the seven years came when no food grew, Joseph could pass food out to the people so they would not starve. The Pharaoh grew to trust Joseph and loved him very much.

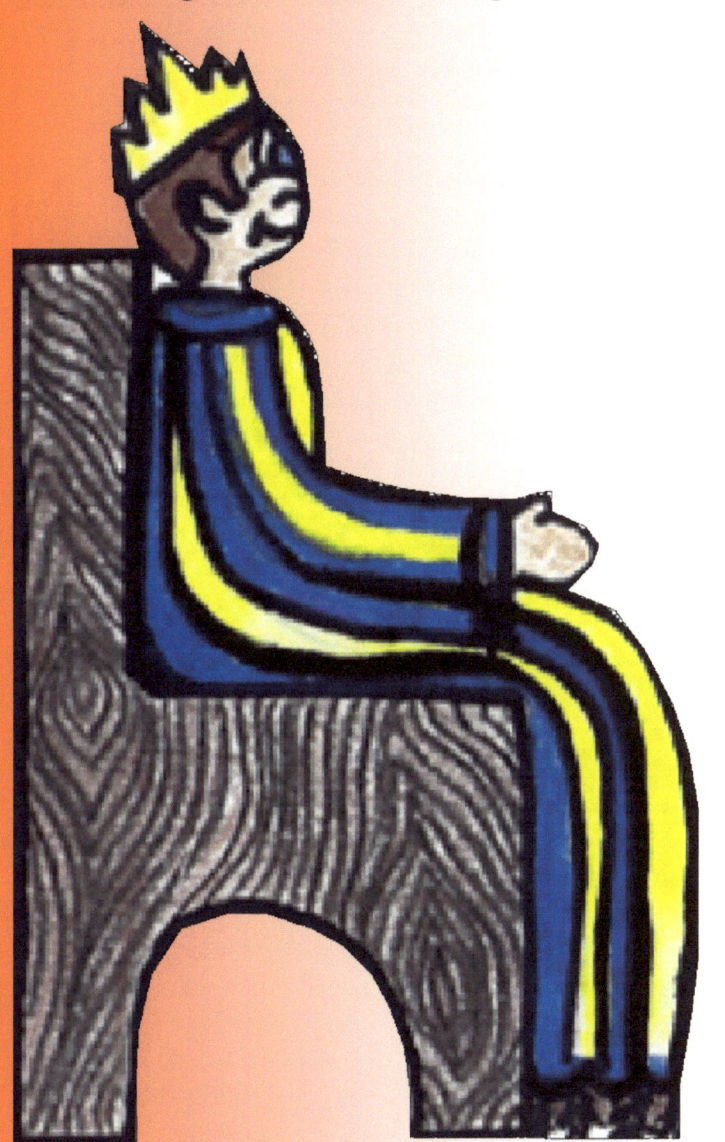

It all happened just as Joseph said it would. The first seven years there was a lot of food growing in the fields. So Joseph saved part of the food every year and when the next seven years came when nothing would grow, Joseph passed out food to the many hungry people.

It was not long before Joseph's own brothers came to him for food. Joseph knew who they were, but his brothers did not know Joseph. By this time Joseph had grown into a man and was no longer the boy his brothers put in the well, or sold to the men who took Joseph to Egypt.

Joseph was so happy to see his brothers that he cried and later told them who he was. He said, "Remember me? Your brother Joseph you threw into the well?" His brothers were very scared, but Joseph told them not to be afraid because it was God's plan to send him to Egypt.

When Pharaoh found out Joseph's family came for food, Pharaoh wanted them all to come and live in Egypt. He gave Joseph's family the best land and all the food and everything they needed.

The brothers then went back and got their father, Jacob. They took him to the new land in Egypt. Joseph went to see his father that he hadn't seen in a long, long time. When they saw each other they cried and cried, they were so happy!

Joseph's family was saved and had many children and lived in the land of Egypt. This family became the huge family God promised Abraham. They were called the Israelites.

God's **First Promise** came true! God said to Abraham, "I will make your family huge, as many as the stars! It happened just as God said!

God's plan is moving right along as Jesus will be coming from Jacob's son Judah!

"Finding God's Plan in His Book"

 This story can be found in the book of Genesis chapters 39-47

 The First Promise was found in Genesis 12:2 and 15:5
It came true in Genesis 46:3

 Jesus was coming from Judah in Luke 3:33

The People God used in His Plan to Bring Jesus!

Adam

⬇

Seth

⬇

Noah

⬇

Shem

⬇

Abraham

⬇

Isaac

⬇

Jacob

⬇

Judah

In a Nut Shell

So far in God's plan to bring Jesus to save us from our sins, Jesus was coming from Adam and Eve's son Seth! Then, God saved Noah from the flood because Jesus was coming from his son Shem! Next, God made **3 promises** to Abraham. **1.** You will have a huge family. **2.** They will live in Canaan. **3.** All people will be blessed through you. Jesus was that blessing! God started the **First Promise** with Abraham, Isaac, Jacob and his 12 sons. Jesus was coming from Judah. Joseph, one of the 12 sons, was put in a well and then taken to Egypt. Joseph tells the Pharaoh what his dream meant and was put in charge of the land and food. Joseph saved his own family from starving during the years when no food grew. Joseph's family moved to Egypt and became the huge family God promised Abraham, and were called the Israelites! The **First Promise** came true in Egypt! Jesus was coming from one of the 12 sons named Judah!

Chapter 7
Moses, the Baby in God's Plan

After the Israelites became the huge family God promised Abraham, a new Pharaoh became the leader in Egypt. He was a very different Pharaoh than the last one. This new Pharaoh was grumpy and did not know about Joseph or how he saved the people from starving.

He also didn't know how much the other Pharaoh loved Joseph and his whole, huge family. This Pharaoh only knew that there were so many Israelites, he was afraid they would take over his land! He wasn't a very kind Pharaoh at all! He was a very selfish man!

The new Pharaoh was such a mean and selfish man he decided to make the Israelites work very hard. They had to do all the work for the people who lived in Egypt first, called Egyptians. God's huge family, the Israelites, worked very, very hard, and were very, very sad!

Not only did Pharaoh make the Israelites work, he also wouldn't let them worship God anymore! Oh no! How horrible that must have been! But this mean Pharaoh **could** not stop God's plan to bring Jesus from the Israelites!

As time went on, the Israelites kept having more and more babies and became an even bigger family of people. This scared Pharaoh even more! So he made a new rule. All the boy babies the Israelites had would be thrown into the river so they would die. He was even meaner than I thought! But the nurses delivering the boy babies would not throw them into the river. They tried to keep them quiet so Pharoah would never know the babies were still alive.

One of the boy baby's name was Moses. Moses' Mama made a basket for him and put him inside. Then she floated the basket safely in the river to hide Moses from Pharaoh. Moses' sister Miriam watched over him as he floated making sure he was safe and snug as a bug! Moses' Mama was a very smart Mama!

Moses floated for awhile and soon a woman spotted him in the basket! But she wasn't just any woman, she was Pharaoh's own daughter! Uh Oh! Miriam thought quickly, and offered to get a woman to be a babysitter for Pharaoh's daughter.

The daughter agreed and Miriam ran and brought their own Mama to be Moses' babysitter! That was a great plan!

As Moses grew bigger and bigger, he continued to live with Pharaoh's daughter. But with his own Mama taking care of him, he knew he was really an Israelite and not an Egyptian. God is going to use Moses in His plan to bring Jesus from this huge family, the Israelites!

Jesus is coming from the Israelite named Judah.

"Finding God's Plan in His Book"

 This story is found in the book of Exodus Chapters 1 and 2

 The **First Promise** was found in Genesis 12:2 and 15:5 It came true in Genesis 46:3

 Jesus is coming from the Israelite named Judah in Luke 3:33

The People God used in His Plan to Bring Jesus!

Adam
⬇
Seth
⬇
Noah
⬇
Shem
⬇
Abraham
⬇
Isaac
⬇
Jacob
⬇
Judah

In a Nut Shell

So far in our story, God planned to send Jesus to save us and Jesus was coming from Seth! When the world was wicked, God saved Noah in the Ark because Jesus was coming from his son Shem! Next, God made **3 promises** to Shem's grandson Abraham. **1.** I will give you a huge family. **2.** I will give them the land of Canaan. **3.** I will bless everyone through you, Abraham. Jesus was the blessing coming from the huge family. The **First Promise** started to come true with Abraham, Isaac, Jacob, and 12 sons. Jesus was coming from the son named Judah. One of the 12 sons named Joseph, whose brothers sold him to men, who took him to Egypt, was all part of God's plan. When Joseph told the Pharaoh what his dream meant, the Pharaoh put Joseph in charge of the land and food because they were going to have a famine. Joseph saved his own family from starving. Pharaoh had them move to Egypt. There, the **First Promise** came true and they became the huge family God promised to Abraham, the Israelites. Jesus was coming from them. Then there was a new Pharaoh who did not like how big the Israelite family had grown. He treated them badly. He wanted to put all the boy babies in the river to drown. A baby named Moses was born and his Mama put him in a basket in the river. Pharaoh's daughter found him and kept him, with Moses' own Mama to be his babysitter. That is how he grew up to know he was really an Israelite.

Chapter 8

Moses, The Man In God's Plan

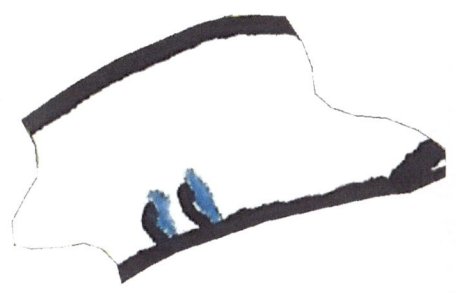

In this puzzle piece of our story Moses grew and grew and soon became a full grown man. God saw how badly the Egyptians were treating His people, the Israelites. God did not like it at all! God wanted Pharaoh to let the Israelites go!

God talked to Moses and said, "Moses, go tell Pharaoh to let my people go!" Moses really did not want to do this because he had a hard time talking. So God sent Moses' brother Aaron with him. Moses and Aaron told Pharaoh that God said to let His people go! Pharaoh looked at Moses and just said, "NO!"

God knew what Pharaoh said and decided to change Pharaoh's mind. The first thing God did was change all of their water in Egypt to blood! Yuck! That would have been horrible! But guess what? When Moses and Aaron went to Pharaoh again and asked to let the Israelites go, Pharaoh said, "NO!"

God continued to challenge Pharaoh's answer. Next, God sent frogs, gnats, and flies to bother Pharaoh and the Egyptians! They were everywhere, in their houses, beds, food and everywhere they walked!

But even that did not work! When Moses and Aaron went to Pharaoh again, Pharaoh still said, "NO!"

This time God made some of their animals die and made sores all over Pharaoh and the Egyptian's bodies. Oh, that must have really hurt! But when Moses and Aaron went to Pharaoh and asked him to let the Israelites go, again he still said, "NO!"

The next time God made it hail everywhere in Egypt! The whole ground was covered in it! Anytime they went outside of their homes they would have been hit by the hail and it would have hurt!

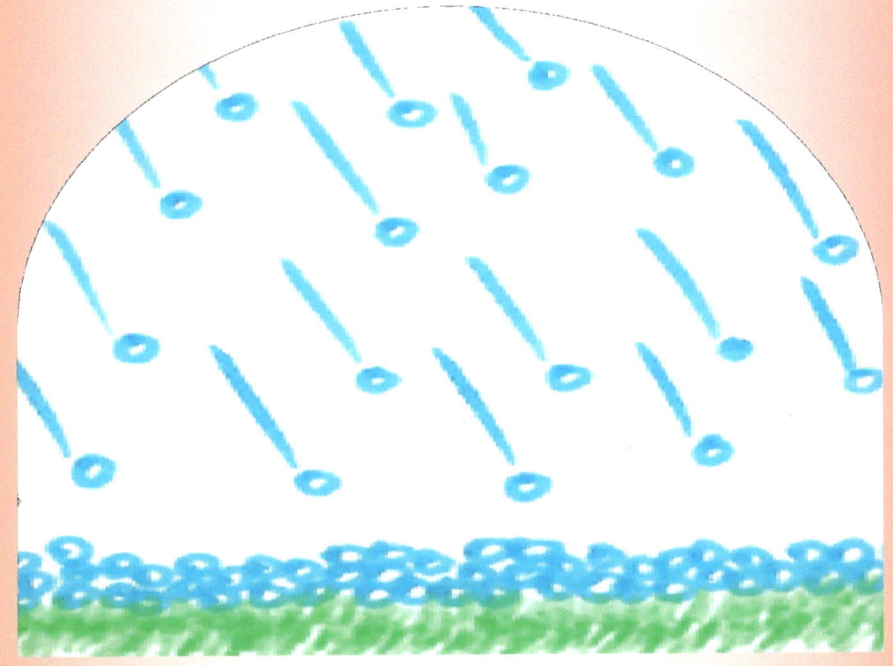

After He sent the hail, God sent grasshoppers! Millions of grasshoppers! Can't you just see them hopping everywhere? They were in their houses, food, and if they walked outside they would have been squished under their feet! Yuck!

But when Moses and Aaron went to Pharaoh he still said, "NO!"

Finally God did one more thing to change Pharaoh's mind to let the Israelites go. This time God struck down the oldest child in each of the Egyptian families including Pharaoh's. Then God struck down the oldest in their animal families. That would have been the most horrible thing God did to them so far!

This time, Pharaoh called Moses and Aron to him and said, "Yes! Go! Take the Israelites, their things, and their animals and leave!" Finally!

YES! GO!

Moses did not waste any time! He gathered everyone together with all their families, the things from their homes, and their animals.

They left that horrible country, Egypt, and that mean Pharaoh! The Israelites were very happy on their journey. I'm sure they were talking and laughing, singing, and dancing! I know I would be!

The Israelites walked and walked until they came to a big body of water called the Red Sea. They all stopped and wondered how they would get across that water! It was then they heard something very loud! They turned around and saw Pharaoh's whole army coming on horses and chariots after them! The Israelites didn't know it but shortly after they left Egypt, Pharaoh had changed his mind and told his army to go bring the Israelites back to Egypt. Oh no! What were they going to do?

They should not have been afraid for they were God's people. God took care of them all this time because Jesus was coming from them! Just then, God said to Moses, "Hold your rod over the water!" Moses did what God said and the water opened up all the way across so they could walk to the other side on dry ground! That was amazing! They did not waste any time and hurried across!

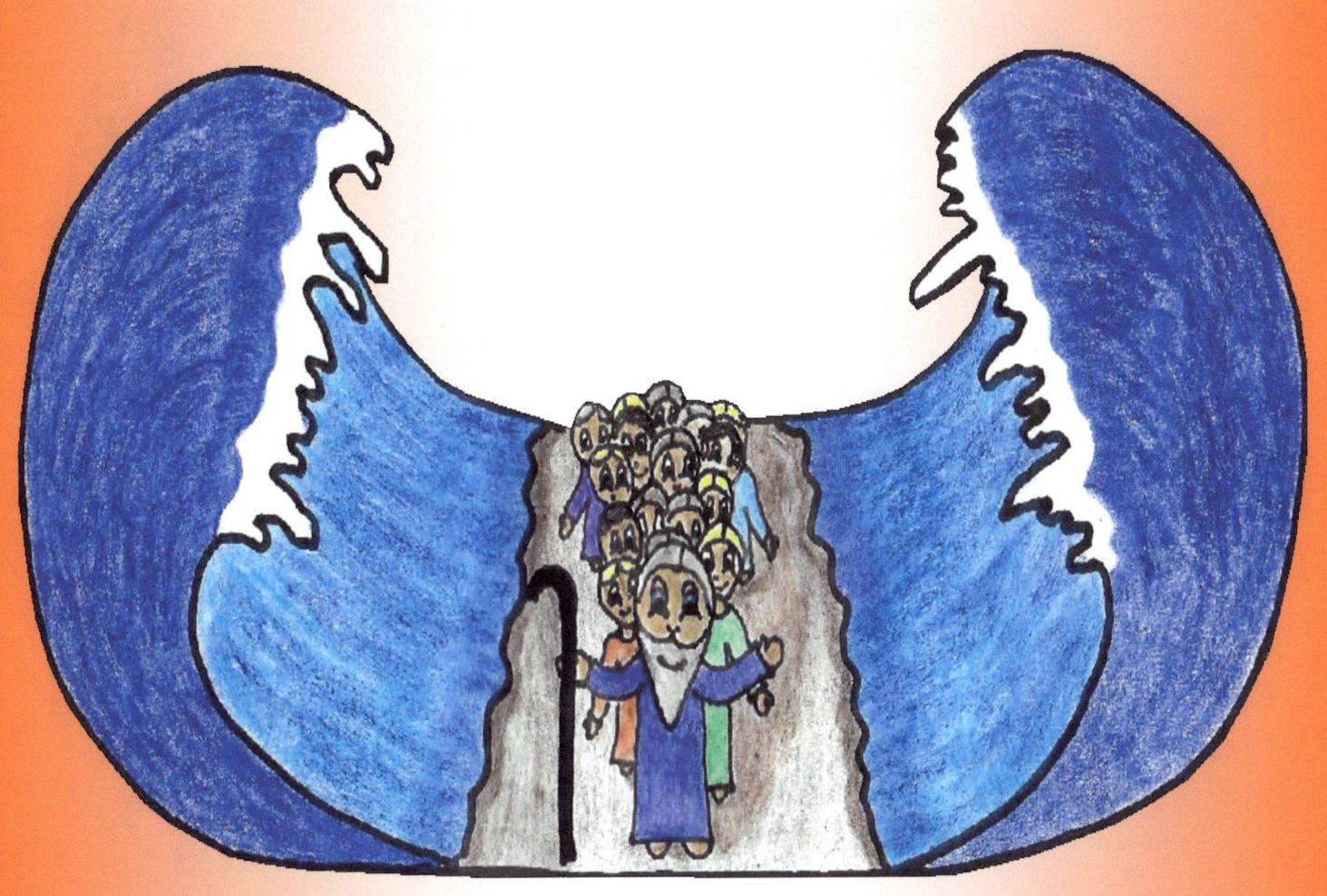

When all the Israelites and their animals finally got across to the other side, Moses looked back and saw Pharaoh's whole army coming across too! Oh No!

God then told Moses to stretch his hand back out over the water. When Moses did as God said, God made the water fall on the whole Egyptian army and they were all drowned!

God did all of this to show the Israelites that He would always take care of them. God used Moses to save this huge family that was the **First Promise** to Abraham who Jesus was coming from.

The Israelites continued on their journey and headed for the Land of Canaan. This was the land God had promised to them in The **Second Promise** to Abraham.

It was during this time that God gave Moses the 10 Commandments. They were rules God gave the Israelites to help them live peaceably with each other and to remind them to keep God most important in their lives.

The Israelites traveled 40 years and God saved them from trouble many, many, times.

It took them such a long time to travel to the land of Canaan that Moses died. After Moses died, God had a man, named Joshua, lead the Israelites. He was a good man and God helped him lead the people just like God helped Moses.

The day finally came and they walked into the land of Canaan! Can you imagine how excited they would have been? Especially after traveling so long to get to the land promised by God to Abraham?

God's **Second Promise** to Abraham came true! "To your huge family, the Israelites, I will give the land of Canaan".

"Finding God's Plan in His Book"

 The Plagues God sent to the Egyptians are found in Exodus chapters 7-12

 Crossing the Red Sea is found in Exodus 13:17– ch.15:21

 The story spans from Exodus 15:22—Joshua 24. There is an entire summary of the story in Joshua 24

 This **Second Promise** from God is in Genesis 12:7 It came true in Joshua 21:43

The People God used in His Plan to Bring Jesus!

Adam
⬇
Seth
⬇
Noah
⬇
Shem
⬇
Abraham
⬇
Isaac
⬇
Jacob
⬇
Judah

In a Nut Shell

In God's plan so far, He is sending Jesus to save us and Jesus was coming from Seth! When the world was wicked, God saved Noah in the Ark because Jesus was coming from his son Shem! Next, God made **3 promises** to Shem's grandson Abraham. **1.** The huge family **2.** The land of Canaan. **3.** The blessing through Abraham. Jesus was the blessing coming from the huge family. The **First Promise** started to come true with Abraham, Isaac, Jacob, and 12 sons. Jesus was coming from the son named Judah. One of the 12 sons named Joseph, whose brothers sold him to men, who took him to Egypt, was all part of God's plan. When Joseph was put in charge of the land and food because they were going to have a famine, Joseph saved his own family from starving. Then Pharaoh had Joseph's family move to Egypt. There, the **First Promise** came true, and they became the huge family God promised to Abraham, the Israelites. Jesus was coming from Judah. Soon there was a new Pharaoh who did not like how big the Israelite family had grown. He wanted to kill all the boy babies. Moses was born and his Mama put him in a basket in the river. Pharaoh's daughter found him and kept him, with Moses' own Mama to be his babysitter. That is how he grew up to know he was really an Israelite. After Moses grew into a man, he lead the Israelites out of Egypt. God did many things to help them along their way to the promised land of Canaan including giving them the 10 Commandments. After many years, God finally gave them the land. The **Second Promise** came true! Jesus was coming from Judah!

Chapter 9
King David In God's Plan

This puzzle piece of our story is about a wonderful man named King David! King David is also a huge part of God's plan to bring Jesus! Let's read and find out how this all happens.

After the Israelites went to live in the Promised land of Canaan, they all built homes for each of their family's. They were very happy for awhile and things were going along smoothly.

Soon, however, they started to notice all the countries around them had leaders called Kings. They had forgotten that God was their greatest king ever! They wanted a king like all the other countries around them. They started pestering God about it. Finally, God told them they could have a king. Through the years to come, they had some kings who loved God and some kings who did not!

One king was a very special king! This special king loved God with all of his heart and God loved this king very much too! His name was King David! King David took very, very, good care of God's people, the Israelites.

King David

King David loved playing his harp and singing! He often played his harp and sang for God! God loved listening to King David play! Can you imagine how beautiful this harp must have sounded?

After King David had been King of the Israelites for a time, he grew to be very lonely. King David finally decided he wanted a wife. He chose to marry a woman named Bathsheba. Bathsheba was a very, very, beautiful woman. She loved King David very much and King David loved Bathsheba very much!

King David   **Bathsheba**

God used King David and his wife Bathsheba in His plan to bring Jesus to the earth to save us from our sins! Jesus was going to be one of King David and Bathsheba's great, great, great, great, grandchildren!

Jesus was coming from King David and Bathsheba

"Finding God's Plan in His Book"

 This story came from the Bible in I Samuel 8 to I Kings 2

 Jesus was coming from David and Bathsheba
Matthew 1:5 and Luke 3:31

The People God used in His Plan to Bring Jesus!

Adam
⬇
Seth
⬇
Noah
⬇
Shem
⬇
Abraham
⬇
Isaac
⬇
Jacob
⬇
Judah
⬇
David and Bathsheba

In a Nut Shell

In God's plan so far, He is sending Jesus to save us and Jesus was coming from Seth! When the whole world was wicked, God saved Noah because Jesus was coming from Shem! Next, God made **3 promises** to Abraham. **1.** The huge family **2.** The land of Canaan. **3.** The blessing through Abraham. Jesus was the blessing. The **First Promise** started to come true with Abraham, Isaac, Jacob, and 12 sons. Jesus was coming from the son named Judah. One of the 12 sons named Joseph ended up in Egypt as part of God's plan. When Joseph was put in charge of the land and food because they were going to have a famine, Joseph saved his own family from starving. They moved there and the **First Promise** came true. They became the huge family God promised to Abraham that Jesus was coming from. Soon there was a new Pharaoh who did not like how big the Israelite family had grown. He wanted to kill all the boy babies. Moses was born and his Mama put him in a basket in the river. Pharaoh's daughter found him and kept him, with Moses' own Mama to be his babysitter. That is how he grew up to know he was really an Israelite. After Moses grew into a man, he lead the Israelites out of Egypt. God did many things to help them along their way to the promised land of Canaan including giving them the 10 Commandments. After many years, God finally gave them the land. The **Second Promise** came true! Jesus was coming from Judah! After the Israelites settled in Canaan they wanted a king. God gave them kings. Some were bad, others were good. King David was one who loved God very much. He chose a wife Bathsheba and Jesus was coming from their great, great grandchildren!

Chapter 10
God's Plan Finally Brought Jesus!

In this part of the puzzle piece of our story, King David and his wife Bathsheba were very happy. They had many babies and two of their children were named Nathan and Solomon. Jesus' Mama was a great, great grandbaby of Nathan and Jesus' Daddy was a great, great grandbaby of Solomon. Those two grandbabies grew and became a man named Joseph and a lady named Mary.

Mary and Joseph were planning to get married. First, however, an angel from God came to talk to Mary. The angel told her she was going to have a boy baby and she should call Him Jesus! The angel said Jesus would be great and called the Son of God!

65

You see, God is Jesus' Father in Heaven and Joseph was Jesus' Daddy on earth.

When Jesus was born, it was the greatest thing that ever happened to us on the earth! Jesus was born in a manger because there was no room for them in the inn. It did not matter where He was born because He was Jesus, God's son!!

This was the **Third Promise** God made to Abraham in the very beginning. God said to Abraham, "All people will be blessed through you." Jesus was coming to save us from our sins! The **Third Promise** finally came true! This is what we have been waiting for all this time in our stories!

"Finding God's Plan in His Book"

 These following verses prove Jesus came from David and Bathsheba's sons, Solomon and Nathan. Joseph's ancestry in Matthew 1:6 and Mary's ancestry in Luke 3:23 (Heli was Mary's father.)

 This story came from the Bible in Luke 2:1-7

 The **Third Promise** to Abraham is in Genesis 12:3 and came true in Galatians 3:8 and 16.

The People God used in His Plan to Bring Jesus!

Adam
↓
Seth
↓
Noah
↓
Shem
↓
Abraham
↓
Isaac
↓
Jacob
↓
Judah
↓
David and Bathsheba
↓
Nathan and Solomon
↓   ↓
Mary   Joseph
↓
Jesus

In a Nut Shell

In God's plan so far, He is sending Jesus to save us and Jesus was coming from Seth! When the world was wicked, God saved Noah because Jesus was coming from Shem! Next, God made **3 promises** to Abraham. **1.** The huge family **2.** The land of Canaan. **3.** The blessing through Abraham. Jesus was the blessing. The **First Promise** started to come true with Abraham, Isaac, Jacob and 12 sons. Jesus was coming from the son named Judah. One of the 12 sons named Joseph ended up in Egypt as part of God's plan. When Joseph was put in charge of the land and food because they were going to have a famine, Joseph saved his own family from starving. They moved there and the **First Promise** came true. They became the huge family God promised to Abraham that Jesus was coming from. Soon there was a new Pharaoh who did not like how big the Israelite family had grown. He wanted to kill all the boy babies. Moses was born and his Mama put him in a basket in the river. Pharaoh's daughter found him and kept him, with Moses' own Mama to be his babysitter. That is how he grew up to know he was really an Israelite. After Moses grew into a man, he lead the Israelites out of Egypt. God did many things to help them along their way to the promised land of Canaan including giving them the 10 Commandments. After many years, God finally gave them the land. The **Second Promise** came true! Jesus was coming from Judah! After the Israelites settled in Canaan they wanted a king. God gave them kings. King David was one who loved God very much. He chose a wife Bathsheba and they had Nathan and Solomon. Mary came from Nathan and Joseph came from Solomon. They grew and were married and they had baby Jesus in a manger. God was Jesus Father in Heaven and Joseph was His Daddy on earth. Jesus was the **Third Promise** to Abraham that came true! All people would be blessed because Jesus had come to take away our sins!

Chapter 11
Jesus Is Baptized by John the Baptist

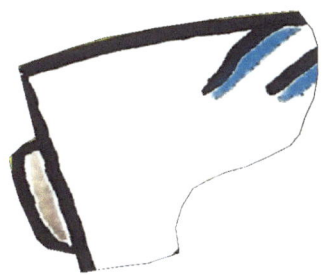

In this puzzle piece of our story Jesus didn't stay a baby very long. Jesus grew and grew and became a full grown man.

When Jesus was about 30 years old, He knew there was a man baptizing people in the Jordan river. This man's name was John the Baptist.

Jesus went to see John the Baptist and wanted to be baptized. John knew who Jesus was and he felt like Jesus should be baptizing him instead. But Jesus told him, "You need to do this to do what is right."

So John took Jesus down into the river. Jesus went down under the water and was baptized.

The meaning of the word "baptism" is to plunge, submerse or totally cover the person in water. That is just what Jesus did.

When Jesus came up out of the water, Heaven opened up and the Spirit of God came on Him like a dove.

Then God, Jesus' Father in Heaven, said, "This is my Son I love, with Him I am well pleased!"

"Finding God's Plan in His Book"

 This story is from the Bible in Mark 1:9-11 and Matthew 3:13-16

"Finding God's Plan in His Book"

The People God used in His Plan to Bring Jesus!

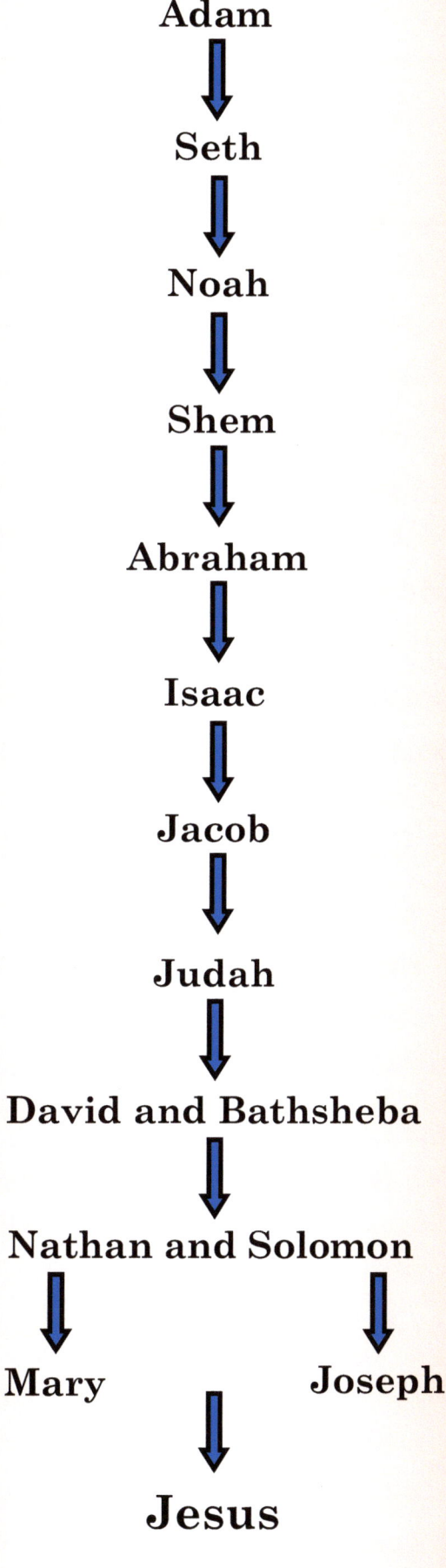

Adam
↓
Seth
↓
Noah
↓
Shem
↓
Abraham
↓
Isaac
↓
Jacob
↓
Judah
↓
David and Bathsheba
↓
Nathan and Solomon
↓   ↓
Mary   Joseph
↓
Jesus

In a Nut Shell

In God's plan so far, He is sending Jesus to save us and Jesus was coming from Seth! God saved Noah because Jesus was coming from his son Shem! Next, God made **3 promises** to Abraham. **1.** The huge family **2.** The land of Canaan. **3.** The blessing through Abraham. Jesus was the blessing. The **First Promise** started to come true with Abraham, Isaac, Jacob and 12 sons. Jesus was coming from the son named Judah. One of the 12 sons named Joseph ended up in Egypt as part of God's plan and saved his own family from starving. They moved there and the **First Promise** came true. They became the huge family God promised that Jesus was coming from. Soon there was a new Pharaoh who did not like how big the Israelite family had grown. He wanted to kill all the boy babies. Moses was born and his Mama put him in a basket in the river. Pharaoh's daughter found him and kept him. With Moses' own Mama as his babysitter he grew up to know he was really an Israelite. Later Moses led the Israelites out of Egypt. God did many things to help them along their way to the promised land of Canaan including giving them the 10 Commandments. After many years, God finally gave them the land and the **Second Promise** came true! Jesus was coming from Judah! After the Israelites settled in Canaan they wanted a king. God gave them kings. King David was one who loved God very much. He chose a wife Bathsheba and they had Nathan and Solomon. Mary came from Nathan and Joseph came from Solomon. They grew and were married and they had baby Jesus in a manger. God was Jesus Father in Heaven and Joseph was His Daddy on earth. Jesus was the **Third Promise** to Abraham that came true! All people would be blessed because Jesus had come to take away our sins! When Jesus grew to be a man, He was baptized by John the Baptist. God told Jesus He was pleased with Him!

Chapter 12

Jesus Chooses Twelve Helpers

In this puzzle piece of our story, after Jesus was baptized, He went around doing many wonderful things for people! Jesus taught them all about God in Heaven and that He was God's Son.

He also taught them to love each other. Jesus taught them many other good things as well. Some of the wonderful things Jesus did was healing a lot of the people that were sick. He healed the blind people so they could see again.

Jesus healed the people who were crippled and couldn't walk. After He healed them, they could walk, run, and jump too!! How happy they were!

It did not matter what was wrong with the people, because Jesus made them all better! Everyone was so grateful to Jesus for the wonderful things He did for them. All of the things Jesus did like this were called, "Miracles!" Jesus was able to do miracles because He was God's Son! Doing miracles helped the people to believe Jesus when He told them who He really was!

After Jesus healed many people, they went to all their friends and people in the cities and told everyone about who Jesus was and what He had done for them!

So many people came to Jesus to be healed of all different kinds of sickness. There were so many people, that soon Jesus wanted helpers to help Him teach and heal even more people.

Jesus walked to many places and as He met different men Jesus asked them to follow Him. As they followed Jesus, He taught them that He was God's Son and had come to save us all from our sins.

There were twelve men who believed everything Jesus taught them. Jesus called them His Apostles. Their names were Peter, James, John, Andrew, Bartholomew, James the younger, Judas, Thaddeus, Matthew, Philip, Simon, and Thomas. Later on Judas was not loyal to Jesus and was replaced by Matthias.

The Apostles went everywhere helping Jesus teach the people. They walked a lot of miles and even went on boats across big lakes. The people were so excited to hear about Jesus, the one they had waited for, such a long, long time! Jesus had finally come to the world to save us from our sins!

"Finding God's Plan in His Book"

 This story is from the Bible in Matthew chapters 4-10, Mark chapters 1-3, Luke chapters 4-9 and John chapters 1-9

The People God used in His Plan to Bring Jesus!

Adam
↓
Seth
↓
Noah
↓
Shem
↓
Abraham
↓
Isaac
↓
Jacob
↓
Judah
↓
David and Bathsheba
↓
Nathan and Solomon
↓ ↓
Mary Joseph
↓
Jesus

In a Nut Shell

In God's plan so far, Jesus was coming from Seth! God saved Noah because Jesus was coming from Shem! Next, God made **3 promises** to Abraham. **1.** The huge family **2.** The land of Canaan. **3.** The blessing through Abraham. Jesus was the blessing. The **First Promise** began with Abraham, Isaac, Jacob, and 12 sons. Jesus was coming from the son named Judah. One of the 12 sons named Joseph was taken to Egypt as part of God's plan and ended up saving his own family from starving. They moved there and became the huge family that Jesus was coming from in the **First Promise** God made. Soon there was a new Pharaoh who did not like how big the Israelite family had grown. He wanted to kill all the boy babies. Moses was born and his Mama put him in a basket in the river. Pharaoh's daughter found him and kept him. With Moses' own Mama as his babysitter he grew up to know he was really an Israelite. Later Moses led the Israelites out of Egypt. God did many things to help them along their way to the promised land of Canaan including giving them the 10 Commandments. After many years, God finally gave them the land and the **Second Promise** came true! Jesus was coming from Judah! After the Israelites settled in Canaan they wanted a king. God gave them kings. King David was one who loved God very much. He chose a wife Bathsheba and they had Nathan and Solomon. Mary came from Nathan and Joseph came from Solomon. They grew and were married and they had baby Jesus in a manger. God was Jesus Father in Heaven and Joseph was His Daddy on earth. Jesus was the **Third Promise** to Abraham that came true! All people would be blessed because Jesus had come to take away our sins! When Jesus grew to be a man, He was baptized by John the Baptist. God told Jesus He was pleased with Him! After Jesus was baptized, He went everywhere teaching the people and doing wonderful things called miracles so they would believe He was God's Son. There were so many people that Jesus chose twelve men to help Him teach even more people. They were so happy to hear about Jesus, the one they had waited to come and save us from our sins!

Chapter 13

Jesus Dies on the Cross and Is Alive Again

In this puzzle piece of our story, Jesus had been teaching the people for a while now. Some of the people loved Jesus and believed everything He taught them. But some of the people did not believe that Jesus was God's Son. They were mad because Jesus kept telling them this. They were so mad they wanted to kill Jesus. How sad for the people who believed and had waited all this time for Jesus to come.

Finally, some of the people were so mad at Jesus they captured Him and planned to hang Him on a wooden cross to die. They wanted to punish Jesus for saying He was God's Son.

After the angry people captured Jesus they hung Him on a wooden cross and stood it up in the ground. That is how Jesus died. The people who loved Jesus so much were very, very, sad.

While Jesus was still on the cross, God made the sky dark and the earth shake! The people who hung Him on that cross were very, very, scared! After that happened they knew then that Jesus was really who He said He was, The Son of God!

The people that hated Jesus and hung Him on that cross, did not know it, but when Jesus died it was all part of God's plan to save us from our sins. God's plan was, that Jesus would die on the cross, be buried, and in three days He would come back to life! God loved us so much He gave His only Son to die to save us from our sins! You know how your parents punish you when you disobey them? Well Jesus took the punishment for our sins on Himself that God would have given us. Our punishment would have been going to a terrible place called Hell.

After Jesus died, a rich man put Him in a place called a tomb to bury Him. They rolled a big rock in front of the door to close the tomb. They were still so sad about Jesus dying. But it happened just as God planned! Three days later, Jesus came back to life. He was alive again! Jesus was going to go back to Heaven to live with God, His Father in Heaven! God made a wonderful plan to save us from our sins!

"Finding God's Plan in His Book"

 A verse describing Hell is Revelation 20:15

 This story comes from the Bible in Matthew 27:45 through chapter 28:6, Mark15:21–chapter 16:6, Luke 23:26-chapter 24:8, John 19:17-chapter 20:18

The People God used in His Plan to Bring Jesus!

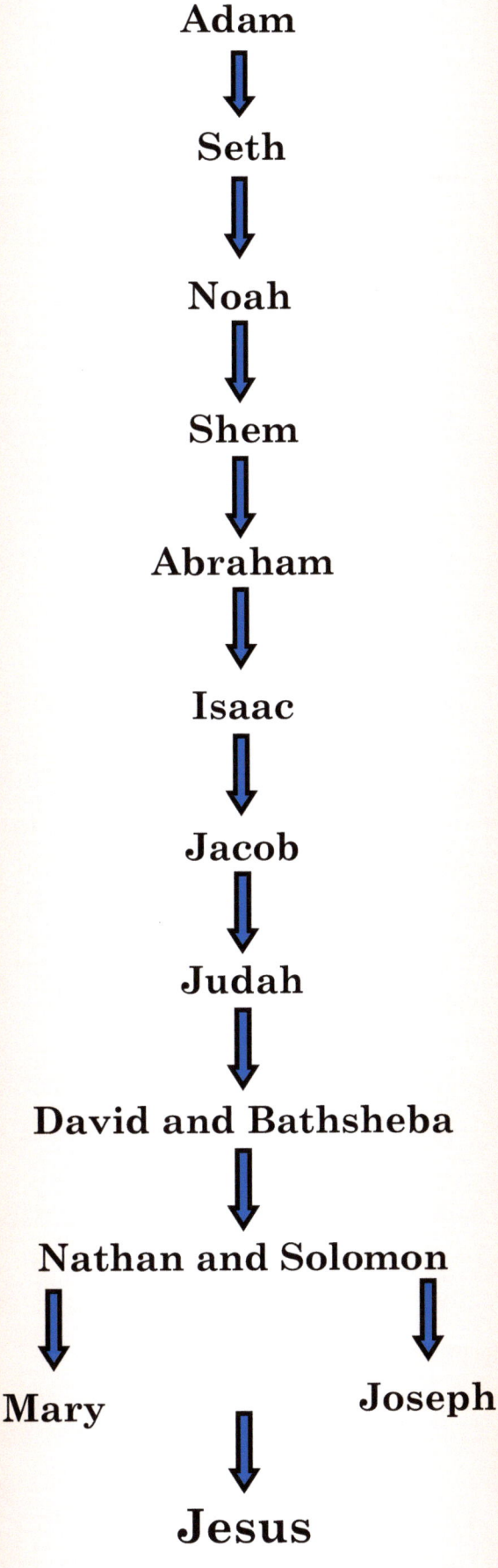

Adam
↓
Seth
↓
Noah
↓
Shem
↓
Abraham
↓
Isaac
↓
Jacob
↓
Judah
↓
David and Bathsheba
↓
Nathan and Solomon
↓   ↓
Mary   Joseph
↓
Jesus

In a Nut Shell

So, this is how God's plan came true. Jesus was coming from Seth! God saved Noah because Jesus was coming from Shem! Next, God made **3 promises** to Abraham. **1.** The huge family **2.** The land of Canaan. **3.** The blessing through Abraham that was Jesus. The **First Promise** began with Abraham, Isaac, Jacob, and 12 sons. Jesus was coming from the son named Judah. One of the 12 sons, named Joseph, was taken to Egypt as part of God's plan and saved the huge family that Jesus was coming from in the **First Promise** God made. Soon there was a new Pharaoh who did not like how big the Israelite family had grown. He wanted to kill all the boy babies. Moses was born and his Mama put him in a basket in the river. Pharaoh's daughter found him and kept him. With Moses' own Mama as his babysitter he grew up to know he was really an Israelite. Later Moses led the Israelites out of Egypt. God did many things to help them along their way to the promised land of Canaan including giving them the 10 Commandments. After many years, God finally gave them the land and the **Second Promise** came true! Jesus was coming from Judah! After the Israelites settled in Canaan, God gave them kings. King David loved God very much. He chose a wife, Bathsheba, and they had Nathan and Solomon. Mary came from Nathan and Joseph came from Solomon. They grew and were married and they had baby Jesus in a manger. God was Jesus Father in Heaven and Joseph was His Daddy on earth. Jesus was the **Third Promise** to Abraham that came true! All people would be blessed because Jesus had come to take away our sins! When Jesus grew to be a man, He was baptized by John the Baptist. God told Jesus He was pleased with Him! After Jesus was baptized, He went everywhere teaching the people and doing wonderful things called miracles, so they would believe He was God's Son. There were so many people Jesus chose twelve men to help Him teach even more people about Jesus, the one they had waited for to come and save us from our sins! However, some of the people were angry when Jesus said He was God's Son; so angry they hung Jesus on a cross. They did not know that this was all part of God's plan that Jesus would die on the cross, be buried, and after three days, come to life again! God gave His Son to save us from our sins!

Chapter 14
The First People In Jesus' Church

In this puzzle piece of our story, Jesus had gone back to Heaven. The people who put Jesus on the cross felt very badly. They finally knew they had crucified Jesus, the Son of God.

Peter, one of Jesus' Apostles, was talking to those people one morning. After listening to Peter explain more about Jesus and who He really was, the people asked him, "What do we do now?"

Peter told them to feel sorry for what they had done to Jesus. Then he said to believe all the things Jesus had taught about God and being His Son. The last thing Peter told them was to be baptized to forgive their sins.

Being baptized is copying what happened to Jesus. Jesus died and was buried, - we are buried and go under the water. Then Jesus raised up from the dead— we are raised up out of the water when we are baptized. God forgives our sins when we are baptized!

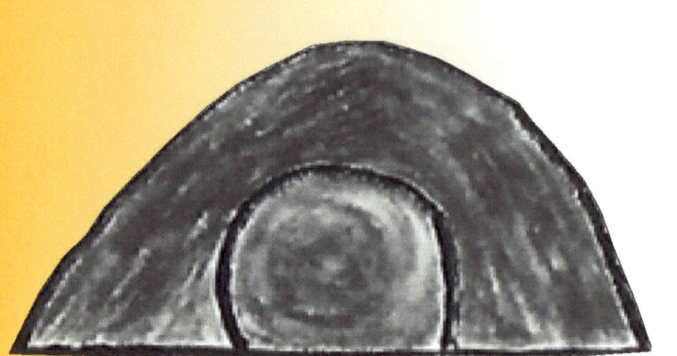

That means if anyone dies after God saves them, and if they keep living the way God wants them to, they would get to live in Heaven forever with God, Jesus and the angels!

That day after Peter told the people they needed to believe in the death, burial, and resurrection of Jesus, repent (in other words feel truly sorry for their sins), confess that Jesus is the Son of God, and be baptized, many of those people did just that. That day there were about 3000 people who were baptized for God's forgiveness of their sins. They were saved!

The people who were baptized that day were the first people in Jesus' church. They were called Christians!

Before Jesus went back to live in Heaven, He told the Apostles to go everywhere teaching people about Him and to baptize people to take away their sins.

Jesus also told the Apostles that He would come and take all the saved people to Heaven with Him to live forever! Isn't God's plan amazing?

When you believe that Jesus was really the Son of God and feel you want to follow Jesus teachings, you can talk to your parents and someday be baptized too!

Now we wait for Jesus to come back and take all of the saved Christians to Heaven to live, forever and ever!

Thank you, God, for loving us so much and for your wonderful plan for Jesus!   In Jesus Name Amen!

"Finding God's Plan in His Book"

 This part of our story is found in the Bible in Acts chapter 2

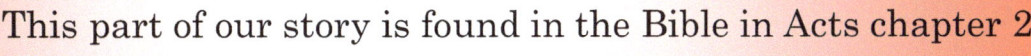 This part of our story is found in the Bible in Matthew 28:18-20

 This part of our story is found in the Bible in I Thessalonians 4:16-18

The People God used in His Plan to Bring Jesus!

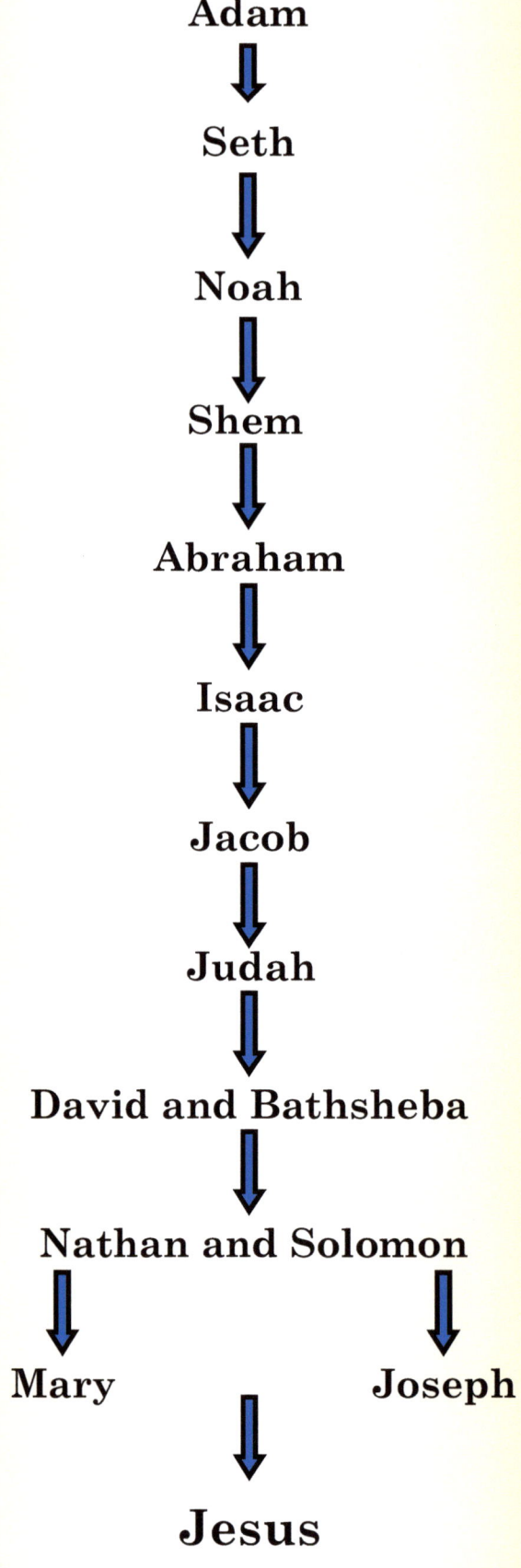

Adam
↓
Seth
↓
Noah
↓
Shem
↓
Abraham
↓
Isaac
↓
Jacob
↓
Judah
↓
David and Bathsheba
↓
Nathan and Solomon
↓   ↓
Mary   Joseph
↓
Jesus

The Puzzle of Jesus! Cut out each piece and put the puzzle together! Enjoy!

www.ingramcontent.com/pod-product-compliance
Lightning Source LLC
Chambersburg PA
CBHW041700160426
43191CB00002B/37